HIDDEN WORLDS
THE INCAS
and MACHU PICCHU

by Philip Steele

DILLON PRESS
New York

First American publication 1993 by Dillon Press, Macmillan Publishing Company, 866 Third Avenue, New York, NY 10022

Macmillan Publishing Company is part of the Maxwell Communication Group of Companies

First published in Great Britain by Zoë Books Limited

A ZOË BOOK

Devised and produced by
Zoë Books Limited
15 Worthy Lane
Winchester
Hampshire SO23 7AB
England

Printed in Italy by Grafedit SpA
Design: Jan Sterling, Sterling Associates
Picture research: Suzanne Williams
Maps: Gecko Limited
Production: Grahame Griffiths

10 9 8 7 6 5 4 3 2 1

Library of Congress Cataloging-in-Publication Data

Steele, Philip.
  The Incas and Machu Picchu / Philip Steele.
    p. cm — (Hidden worlds)
  Includes index.
  Summary: Discusses Hiram Bingham's 1911 expedition in search of the lost city of the Incas and describes how he came to find Machu Picchu.
  ISBN 0-87518-536-3
  1. Machu Picchu Site (Peru) — Juvenile literature.
2. Incas — Juvenile literature. 3. Bingham, Hiram, 1875-1956 — Juvenile literature. [1. Machu Picchu Site (Peru) 2. Bingham, Hiram, 1875-1956. 3. Incas. 4. Indians of South America.] I. Title. II. Series.
F3429.1.M3S74 1993
985'.37—dc20   92-42283

Photographic acknowledgments
The publishers wish to acknowledge, with thanks, the following photographic sources:

The Hutchison Library: 12/Eric Lawrie; Marion and Tony Morrison, South American Pictures: title page, 5, 6, 10, 14, 15t & b, 16t & b, 17t & b, 18, 19t & b, 20t & b, 21, 22t & b, 23, 24t & b, 25b, 26t & b, 27, 28t & b; Courtesy of the National Geographic Society, photographs taken by Hiram Bingham or under his direction and reproduced in the *National Geographic Magazine*, April 1913: 7t & b, 8t & b, 9, 11b;© Yale University, Peabody Museum of Natural History/Syndication International: 25t; Zefa: cover/Kurt Goebel, 11t/Hed Weisner, 29/J Schörken

10,651

Contents

Children of the sun

Peru is a country in South America, beside the waters of the Pacific Ocean. Near its coast there are low-lying deserts, but inland lie the high, snowy peaks of the Andes Mountains. Beyond these mountains are dense tropical forests and a maze of rivers that drain into the mighty Amazon River.

Between about 3,000 and 500 years ago, several **civilizations** grew up in ancient Peru. The greatest was that of the Incas.

▶ The power of the Incas was at its greatest between the years 1493 and 1525. The **empire** stretched almost 2,500 miles along the Pacific coastline and about 200 miles inland. Its power extended into the lands now known as Colombia, Ecuador, Chile, Bolivia, and Argentina. A network of roads linked the main towns of the empire.

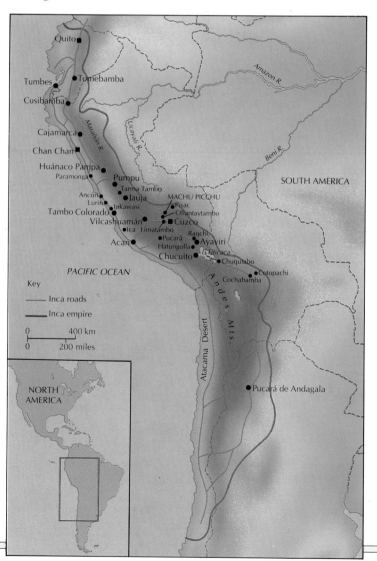

The Inca people settled in the Cuzco region, high in the Andes, about 900 years ago. In A.D. 1438 the Inca ruler, Pachacuti Inca Yupanqui, built up a powerful state around Cuzco. His son conquered the powerful Chimu people so that vast areas of land became part of an Inca empire.

Peru was soon torn apart by **civil war**. In 1532 the ruler Huáscar was overthrown by his brother Atahualpa. More trouble was to come. Stories of the Inca empire and its fabulous wealth had spread to distant Europe. These rumors said that the Inca rulers wore gold and were descended from the sun itself.

No sooner had Atahualpa become emperor than a small force of Spanish soldiers arrived in Peru, led by Francisco Pizarro. They were greedy for gold and wanted to conquer the country for themselves.

Pizarro captured Atahualpa and demanded a high **ransom** for him. Although the Incas paid the Spanish soldiers a fortune, the Spaniards put the Inca ruler to a cruel death.

Many Incas fought bravely against the Spanish until 1572, but the Europeans were in South America to stay. The greatest empire of ancient Peru was to be the last.

◀ The Spanish entered the town of Cajamarca in November 1532. They were received by Atahualpa. When he was shown the Bible, he cast it aside. Many Incas believed that the Spanish had been sent by the sun god. In fact they had to come to kill. The Spanish massacred 7,000 Inca warriors at Cajamarca and murdered Atahualpa the following summer.

In search of the lost city

Spanish rule was harsh. The peoples of the former Inca empire worked on the land and in the mines. They became very poor, while the Europeans became very rich.

The Inca temples were stripped of their gold and destroyed. Graves were broken into and any precious objects they contained were stolen and sold. The treasures of a great civilization were being destroyed or lost. The forest began to grow back over many Inca towns. Plants crept over the ruined stone walls.

It was not until the 1800s that people around the world began to realize that such treasures should be preserved. Ancient sites were dug up, or **excavated**, and their remains were studied scientifically. A new interest in **archaeology** grew up.

▼ Machu Picchu lies on a ridge 8,000 feet above the Urubamba River. Rising in the Andes, the Urubamba flows through steep gorges for 445 miles before it joins with the Apurímac to form the great Ucayali River.

The first expedition

In 1911 Dr. Hiram Bingham, an American archaeologist, came to Peru from Yale University. Bingham was fascinated by the lost world of the Incas. He had read how the Incas had made a final stand against the Spanish at a place called Vilcabamba. Perhaps he could find the ruins of their last stronghold. Bingham traveled to Cuzco, the old Inca capital.

From Cuzco he followed a mule track to a remote area 60 miles to the north. On the sixth day he came to a small plantation called Mandor Pampa. Here, an old man offered to guide the American to some hidden ruins.

A dangerous-looking bridge of logs took the explorers across the rushing white waters of the Urubamba River. They began to climb a steep path through the forest. The twin mountains of Machu Picchu and Huayna Picchu towered above them, and soon the river lay far below.

Hiram Bingham could see traces of terraced fields, or **andenes**. Suddenly, he could scarcely believe his eyes. Ahead of the guide a maze of ruined walls appeared, covered in roots and plants. Here, amid the high peaks of the Andes, was surely one of the most breathtaking sites in all the Americas!

▲ In the 1900s the countryside around Machu Picchu was still very wild. This mule track on the banks of the Urubamba River had only just been opened up. It led Hiram Bingham to a vanished world.

◀ Hiram Bingham took this photograph of Machu Picchu after spending ten days clearing the undergrowth. The impressive ruins were beginning to emerge from the jungle.

Return to Machu Picchu

▲ All the expedition's heavy equipment had to be carried along the trail by mules or by people. In 1912 the archaeologists could not use helicopters or four-wheel-drive vehicles, as they might today.

► Kenneth Heald was the expedition's pioneer. He went ahead of the main party and lashed together this bridge over the rapids of the Urubamba River.

Hiram Bingham returned to the United States full of enthusiasm. He was determined to map and excavate this lost city of the Incas. He planned a second expedition, with the support of Yale University and the *National Geographic Magazine*.

Bingham's first job was to find a team of experts. He needed other archaeologists who could help him. He also needed a geographer to help prepare maps of the area. Bingham knew that if he found human remains, the bones would help him to date the site and to find out how it had been used by the Incas. So he recruited a bone specialist, an **osteologist**, for the expedition.

The expedition assembled in Peru and on July 12, 1912, Kenneth Heald, Bingham's assistant, set out from Cuzco. His job was to prepare a route for the others. Heald built a new bridge across the Urubamba River, to the east of the Machu Picchu site. He then cut a trail through thickets of bamboo. In many places he had to clear away the dense undergrowth by burning it.

At last the way was open. Bingham set out, his porters carrying the boxes of precious supplies. They crossed the Urubamba and toiled up to the ridge, where they set up camp.

Bingham's first job was to **survey** the site. He needed to know more about the lay of the land and to map the boundaries of the site. The settlement had been built at 12,000 feet above sea level, and covered about 100 acres.

Kenneth Heald was sent to climb the peak of Huayna Picchu. Scrambling up the mountainside, he nearly plunged to his death. Luckily he survived and reached the top on a second attempt. There was only a small ruined building there, perhaps an Inca lookout post. It seemed that the main site was on the lower ridge, or **saddle**, between the two peaks, Huayna Picchu and Machu Picchu.

◄ Hiram Bingham in the expedition's camp at Machu Picchu. He was sure that the site had played an important part in Inca history.

Archaeologists at work

The archaeologists now began the hard work. As they hacked the undergrowth away, it became clear that the ancient stonework had survived very well. Where large trees had rooted in the walls, however, there were problems. There were fears that removing the tree roots might break up the **masonry**.

Buildings were mapped and measured. Some houses had been so cleverly constructed that Hiram Bingham called them the "Ingenuity" group. The stones fitted together so well that they did not need **mortar** to hold them in place.

Excavations began in two promising places, the Principal Temple and the Temple of the Three Windows. Trenches were dug to depths of up to about 10 feet. To Bingham's disappoint-

▼ The Temple of the Three Windows was examined by Hiram Bingham during his first expedition. The "windows" were three large openings in a massive stone wall. Bingham recalled an ancient Inca legend. It told how the Incas of Cuzco had first come from a place called *Tampu Tocco*, which means "tavern of the windows."

ment, nothing was found at these sites. He had hoped to find objects, or **artifacts**, made by the Incas.

Inca burials

Some 101 burial sites were discovered, mostly in natural caves on the slopes beneath the city. A few were in hollowed-out chambers in the city itself. One site was about 1,000 feet above the city, beneath a rock. Each site was carefully photographed, drawn, and measured.

The skeletons of the Incas had been buried as if they were sitting with their knees drawn up. Artifacts were buried with them. There were pots, tweezers, shawl pins, and a knife and mirror made of bronze. There were traces of wool and vegetable fiber, all that remained of the people's clothing.

The archaeologists found a total of 173 skeletons. Hiram Bingham was puzzled, because 150 of these were females, who seemed to have been wealthy. An old legend in Peru said that the High Priestess and the holy women, or *mamacuna*, had fled from Cuzco during the Spanish invasion. Might they have come here, to Machu Picchu?

▲ This cave at Machu Picchu has a triangular entrance. Its steps are cut out of solid rock. The Incas used caves as burial places.

◄ This photograph was taken by Hiram Bingham. A team of local workers is excavating the site of the main temple in Machu Picchu.

The city revealed

The archaeologists at Machu Picchu uncovered a mountain stronghold built from blocks of a hard, white rock called **granite**. Perched on the mountain ridge, the city could be approached from one side only. It was defended by a double wall and a dry ditch, or moat. The wooden city gates were unlocked to allow people in and out. On the outskirts of the city the soldiers lived in **barracks**.

The city was built on rising ground, so the buildings were at various heights. Some were built into solid rock, but most were on terraces made of stone blocks. The steep streets included 100 stone stairways, each with up to 100 steps. Water was supplied by the mountain springs of Machu Picchu, a mile away. The water was carried to the city along an **aqueduct** and was channeled to the houses, fountains, and gardens.

At the center of the city was the Great Plaza. This was where public announcements were made.

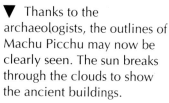

▼ Thanks to the archaeologists, the outlines of Machu Picchu may now be clearly seen. The sun breaks through the clouds to show the ancient buildings.

The Incas believed that the sun god was the most important of all the gods. The holiest part of the city was probably the Sun Stone, the *Intihuatana*. Temples were built on high ground, and the palaces of the nobles were nearby.

In the outer parts of Machu Picchu were the houses of farmers, laborers, and crafts workers. Here there were public storehouses for food and other supplies.

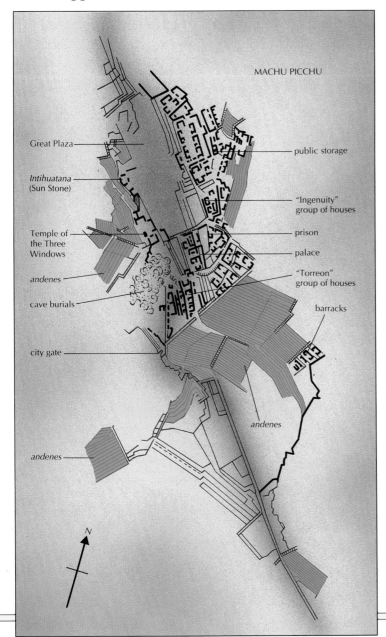

MACHU PICCHU

Great Plaza

Intihuatana
(Sun Stone)

Temple of
the Three
Windows

andenes

cave burials

city gate

public storage

"Ingenuity"
group of houses

prison

palace

"Torreon"
group of houses

barracks

andenes

andenes

N

◄ About 1,000 people lived in Machu Picchu. It was much smaller than Cuzco. It was built about 500 years ago, when Inca power was at its height.

Rulers and ruled

The remains at Machu Picchu have helped historians piece together the details of how the Incas lived from day to day. As the buildings were cleared of plants and bushes, it became obvious that the houses of the nobles were separated from the more humble dwellings. Inca society was divided into strict **social classes**. The city was also divided into groups of families or **clan** areas. The members of each clan, or *ayllu*, were usually descended from the same ancestor.

▶ Archaeology can tell us how people lived in ancient times. In Machu Picchu the houses of the nobles were at the center of the town, away from the houses of the ordinary people.

At the top of the social order was the emperor, or *Sapa Inca*. In the later period of Inca power, the emperor married one of his own sisters. She became the empress, or *Coya*. The emperor also had hundreds of less important wives, who were chosen from the most beautiful girls in the empire.

The many children born to the emperor all became nobles. The men worked as regional governors, priests, judges, and army officers. The chiefs of the tribes that were conquered by the Incas could also keep their high rank, if they promised to be loyal to the emperor and to worship the sun.

For the lower classes, everyday life was made up of hard work. Crops and other products had to be given to the public stores. In Machu Picchu the storehouses were situated in the north of the city. Goods were then handed out according to need, and officials made sure that the elderly and the infirm were given their share of food and clothing.

Running the empire

The government was very efficient. The emperor's wishes were carried out by the four officers, or **prefects**, of the Supreme Council. Each prefect represented one quarter of the empire. The Inca name for Peru was *Tahuantinsuyu*, or "the four quarters" (north, south, east, and west).

Money was not used in ancient Peru, so **taxes** were paid in the form of crops, labor, or military service. Nobles and officials did not have to pay taxes. The number of people in each town was counted regularly. The Incas used a system of counting off in groups of ten.

Machu Picchu had a prison to the southwest of the Great Plaza. Laws were strict and punishments were severe.

▼ The *Sapa Inca* ruled from Cuzco, but he traveled around the empire with the *Coya*. This picture was drawn in the 1600s by Guaman Poma de Alaya. It shows the famous emperor Topa Inca Yupanqui, who ruled from 1471 to 1493.

▼ Workers carry sacks of grain into the public storehouse. Ordinary people were not allowed to travel around the empire. They had to stay at home and work in the fields. Some were sent to live in lands that had been conquered by the Inca armies.

Priests and warriors

▶ The Sun Stone, or *Intihuatana*, casts a shadow at Machu Picchu. It recorded the movement of the sun across the sky. The Incas worshiped both the sun and the moon and their children — the stars.

▲ This gold mask is made in the shape of the sun, the god of the *Sapa Inca*. It was treasure such as this that attracted the Spanish soldiers to Peru.

Machu Picchu had many fine temples. There were also places where people were killed as an offering or sacrifice to the gods and goddesses. To the east of the Great Plaza, Hiram Bingham discovered the great rock of the Sun Stone, or *Intihuatana*.

The Incas believed that a god called Viracocha was the maker, or **creator**, of the world, the sun, and the moon. On earth, the Inca emperor represented the sun god, *Inti*. The empress represented the moon goddess, *Mama-quilla*. The thunder god, *Illapa*, was the messenger of the sun. The harvest was looked after by the earth mother, *Pacha-mama*, and on the coast, fishing people worshiped *Mama-cocha*, the sea goddess.

The Incas worshiped at temples and also at local holy places, or shrines, called *huacas*. Holy places and objects included stones, springs, tombs, and caves. There were men and women priests. Some girls were chosen to become *mamacuna*, or the unmarried *acllas*. They vowed to live a religious life and to serve in the temples.

The most important worship was of the sun god, and this fact helped to make the emperor all–powerful. He was not only the religious head of his people, but the commander in chief of the Inca armies.

Armies of the sun

Army officers were trained at an early age. The serving soldiers were fed from storehouses that were set up in every corner of the empire. Troops were well drilled and fought with spears, swords, and axes made of bone, stone, hardened wood, or copper. They also had bows and arrows, clubs and maces, slings, and *bolas* (three stones tied to a long string). Shields and helmets were made of wood, and armor was made of thick pads of cotton.

Different ranks in the army wore various badges and headdresses. Armies went into battle with colorful standards and played drums and flutes sometimes made from the skin and bones of their enemies. However, the lives of defeated enemy soldiers were often spared.

▲ Nobles from Machu Picchu may have traveled to Cuzco for *Inti Raymi*, the great festival of the sun. There would be dancing, feasting, and sacrifices to the sun god.

◄ Today, people in Cuzco keep alive the great festival of the sun, or *Inti Raymi*. In Inca times nobles from Machu Picchu probably traveled to Cuzco each year in order to feast, dance, and make sacrifices to the sun god.

Science–and magic

▲ The plant with the yellow flower is called calceolaria. It was used in a medicine that cured infections. In Inca times, a person who was skilled at curing sick people was called a *hampi camayoc*. As in Europe during this time, medicine was a mixture of genuine cures and superstitions.

The Incas were skilled doctors and surgeons. They made healing or pain-killing drugs such as **quinine**, tobacco, and **coca** from herbs and the bark of trees or from the leaves of forest plants. They were also able to operate on people's skulls. The Incas believed that magic was the cause of most sickness. Treatments often included religious ceremonies, or **rituals**, which were intended to drive out evil spirits.

The Incas had little resistance to common European illnesses such as measles. After the Spanish invasion, many Inca people became ill and died.

The sun, moon, and stars played an important part in the religious beliefs of the Incas. They studied how the stars and planets moved around, which is called **astronomy**. They also worked out a calendar to help to decide when to plant their crops.

Arithmetic was based on a **decimal system**. Counting frames were divided into twenty sections, each containing seeds or pebbles. The cleverest way of counting was by using a system of knotted cords called *quipus*.

Education

The ordinary people of Machu Picchu learned the skills of farming, weaving, or building from their parents. The emperors claimed that too much education was bad for ordinary working people.

Girls chosen to serve in the temples as mamacuna or acllas were educated in special schools or **convents**. The sons of nobles were sent to school in Cuzco, where they studied religion, poetry, *quipu*, arithmetic, history, and Quechua, which was the main language of the Inca empire.

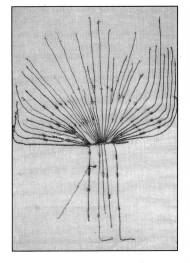

▲ The *quipu* was made up of a cord tied with strings. The knots tied in the strings formed a code.

◄ People were trained to use the *quipu* for taking the **census** or for keeping accounts. *Quipus* were also used to help people remember long lists of historical events or religious rituals. At the bottom of the picture on the left is a counting frame.

Builders and engineers

The blocks of granite at Machu Picchu were shaped until they fitted together exactly. Roof beams were tied to the stone pegs.

The archaeologists discovered that the granite walls of Machu Picchu were built by experts. The Incas did not use mortar to cement the blocks together, but today the edges still fit together so closely that a knife blade cannot be pushed in between. The walls lock together so well that even if they are shaken by an earthquake they often fall back into position.

The people who planned the buildings, the **architects**, were nobles. They used small working models made of stone. The laborers were ordinary people, who worked as a means of paying their taxes. They cut the blocks of stone from the quarries and shaped them, smoothing down the surface with sand and water. The stones were moved by rolling them along on logs. They were raised with ramps and bronze **crowbars**.

Most buildings had only one level, or **story**. Buildings with two stories were linked by rope

▶ Stone steps lead past a house at Machu Picchu. The building has been thatched with *ichu* grass to show how it would have looked 500 years ago.

ladders or by stepping stones set in the outer wall. At Machu Picchu, the roofs sloped steeply, so that the water would run off during heavy rainstorms.

Roads and bridges

At the time of the Spanish invasion of Peru, roads in Europe were little more than muddy tracks. However in the Inca empire the roads were built by experts. There were more than 10,000 miles of road, and much of it was paved. Stone or rope bridges were built across rivers and gorges. Stone markers recorded the distance in *topos*, which were units of about 6 miles. The Incas built rest houses and public stores by the roadside. There were huts for officials and for the relay runners who carried messages to and from the emperor.

Nobles were carried around in handheld carriages without wheels, called **litters**. Surprisingly, the Incas did not know how to make wheels. Goods were carried by people or on the backs of **llamas**, animals still used today in the Andes.

The harvest and the hunt

▶ The terraced fields were filled with good soil. Their walls prevented the precious earth from being washed away by the rain or blown off the mountainside by the wind.

▼ *Quinoa* ripens in the Peruvian Andes. This was grown as a food crop by Inca farmers.

The stone walls of the terraced fields, the *andenes*, at Machu Picchu, have survived for more than 400 years. They show clearly how much the Incas depended on farming.

The most important crops in the mountains were potatoes, a root crop called *oca*, and a grain called *quinoa*. In lowland regions and in the warmer mountain valleys, corn was widely grown. This was ground into flour and made into loaves, dumplings, porridge, and a kind of beer called *chicha*.

Farmers broke up the soil with digging sticks called *tacllas* and weeded with hoes made of bronze. Llama dung and sewage were used as manure. Fish meal and seabird droppings, called *guano*, were sometimes brought to the fields from the coast. This helped to fertilize the land. The Incas were skilled at building channels to carry water over their farmland to **irrigate** the crops.

Some land was said to "belong to the gods." Other land belonged to the emperor. These fields had to be sown and harvested before the people could work on the land that was for their own use.

Little meat was eaten in Machu Picchu. The farmers and their families raised and ate guinea pigs. The nobles fed upon fish and birds and on tropical fruits such as bananas, which were transported along the roads around the empire. Herds of llamas were grazed on mountain pastures. They were sometimes eaten but were mostly kept for their wool or for transporting goods.

Hunting

Royal officials arranged hunts at certain times, when the people were allowed to hunt with nets and bolas. They killed dangerous wild animals such as bears, and caught deer, rabbits, partridges, and a wild llama called a *guanaco*. The meat was shared out and cut into strips. These would be dried in the sun so that they would not spoil. The meat strips were cooked with vegetables to make stews.

◀ Potato pickers lay out their crop to dry in the sunshine of the Peruvian Andes. The scene may have looked much the same about 500 years ago. The potato grows well in mountain regions and was first grown in the Americas.

Bronze, gold, and feathers

▶ This fine cloak, or poncho, was woven by Inca women. Dyes for the thread were made from plants. When the Spanish king and queen first saw Inca cloth, they marveled at its softness and fine quality.

▼ This drinking vessel is made from wood. It is shaped like a jaguar, the fierce big cat of the South American rainforests.

Crafts workers in the Inca empire were employed by the government. They did not have to pay taxes like the laborers. The Incas had no iron, but they were experts at working with gold, silver, platinum, tin, and copper. Tin and copper were melted together to make the mixture, or **alloy**, bronze.

Large amounts of tin were used for shaping, or **casting**, bronze. Smaller amounts were used to make the kind of bronze that was beaten into knives, axes, or other tools. Small furnaces called **braziers** were discovered by archaeologists at Machu Picchu. These had been used for

producing bronze and still contained traces of molten metals.

Many stone tools were also found at Machu Picchu. Some tools were used for working and polishing decorative stones, such as the green **schist** that the Incas used for making dishes and jewelry.

Llama bones were used to make all kinds of objects, from needles to spoons and flutes. Pottery was made of clay that was often mixed with sand or shells. It was not made on a potter's wheel, but was built up in coils or, in parts of the empire, shaped by molds. Pots were often shaped in human or animal form. Patterns were painted or scraped on the pots.

Clothes and jewelry

Few materials or **textiles** survived in the damp mountain air at Machu Picchu. In the desert regions of Peru, Inca cloth was better preserved. On the coast, cotton was grown. In the Andes, wool was taken from llamas to make coarse blankets, and from similar animals called *vicuñas* and *alpacas* to make finer cloth. All kinds of spinning and weaving tools were discovered at Machu Picchu. Tunics, cloaks, belts, and headbands were woven and dyed.

Sandals were made from leather or from plaited plant fibers. Both men and women wore jewelry, and noblemen wore large gold earplugs as badges of their rank. Feathers were used to decorate cloaks, collars, and headdresses.

◀ This bronze knife, or *tumi*, was found at Machu Picchu. It was used in Inca ceremonies. It is decorated with a boy catching a fish.

▼ This little *alpaca* is made from solid silver. These animals are still bred for their fine wool.

Everyday life

▶ This is how Machu Picchu must have looked 500 years ago. Life was spent farming, cooking, and weaving. Men would leave home from time to time to work in one of the public services — in the army or the mines or on a building site.

▼ The Incas used pottery jugs to carry water from the fountains into their houses.

The ordinary houses at Machu Picchu were dark inside. They were drafty, too, for they had no doors. Entrances were hung with a cloth. Small clay stoves provided warmth in cold weather.

Archaeologists have found no traces of wooden furniture. It may have rotted away, or perhaps the Incas did not use wood for furniture. There was a stone bench, and possessions were arranged on shelves or **niches** set in the walls or hung on stone pegs. Food and water were kept in large pots. People slept on the floor, on mats made of reeds.

Cooking and weaving took place in the outer courtyards. Here, people could meet other members of their clan. Stone channels and fountains provided spring water for washing and bathing.

Children helped their parents with everyday chores. Men worked very hard and women even harder, for they were expected to do the housework as well as helping in the fields.

However, there was more to life than work. Ordinary people, as well as nobles, loved to drink, dance, play games, tell stories, and make music.

Musical instruments included flutes, whistles, drums, bells, rattles, and **panpipes** made of bamboo cane. There were many family celebrations and public festivals.

Getting married

Each year a royal official called together all the unmarried men and women in town. Marriages were arranged by him. Men were usually married by the time they were 25 years old and women by the age of twenty. Weddings were a time for gifts and feasting. A special house was prepared for each newly married couple. The couple did not have to pay any taxes for a year.

When a baby was born, the parents received extra land from the government. Babies were placed in a movable wooden cradle, or *quirau*. This could be placed on the ground or carried on the mother's back.

◀ All over the Inca empire people loved to play pipes, drums, and other musical instruments. There was dancing on public holidays.

Past, present, and future

▲ Vilcabamba was discovered by American archaeologist Gene Savoy in 1964. The lost city of the Incas was located in the Peruvian jungle. It was not high on a mountainside like Machu Picchu.

Hiram Bingham returned to Peru on a final expedition in 1914. He continued to lecture to students at Yale University until 1924 and later became a United States senator. He died in 1956.

Many other archaeologists followed Bingham to Peru. Some returned to Machu Picchu. Others excavated sites in the coastal deserts and in the jungles beyond the mountains. Later archaeologists were helped by new technology and new methods of working. They could survey and photograph sites from the air. They could find out the age of cloth, bones, and plant remains by a method called **radiocarbon dating**.

More and more has been revealed about the Incas and about the wondrous civilizations that came before them—the Chavin and Moche cultures and the empires of Tiahuanaco and Huari. The Spanish destroyed more than the Inca empire. They destroyed over 3,000 years of Peruvian civilization.

Yet the traditions of the ancient Peruvians have not been completely forgotten. About three million Quechua people live in modern Peru. They take their name from, and speak, the

▶ A market scene in modern Peru. The Quechua people have not forgotten the empire of the Incas. For many farmers in remote mountain areas, life has changed little over the ages.

ancient Inca language. Their lives have much in common with those of their ancestors. They harvest potatoes or corn, play the panpipes, and weave colorful textiles. Ancient Inca ceremonies are proudly reenacted in Cuzco, the capital of the ancient empire.

Much has changed. An international airport has now been built in Cuzco, and trains take tourists up the valley of the Urubamba River. A road twists and turns up to the ridge of Machu Picchu.

However, the site is as spectacular as ever. The fact that this was just one small part of the mighty Inca empire makes it all the more impressive. If you forget the tourists and the cameras, it is easy to imagine life in the Andes 500 years ago. One can imagine the children playing on the steps, the officials from Cuzco busily checking the public stores, and the priests, glittering with gold, making a sacrifice to the sun.

◀ Machu Picchu, high among the peaks of the Urubamba gorge, has fascinated the world ever since its discovery over 80 years ago.

ST. THOMAS THE APOSTLE

Glossary

alloy: a mixture of two or more metals.

andene: a terraced field built into the mountainside.

aqueduct: any channel built to carry water over a long distance, often raised above the ground.

archaeology: the scientific study of ancient remains.

architect: a person who designs buildings.

artifact: any object made and used by people.

astronomy: the scientific study of the night sky.

barracks: buildings where soldiers are housed.

brazier: a container of burning fuel used as a stove or furnace.

casting: pouring molten metal into a mold.

census: a count of the population.

civil war: a war that takes place between rival groups within one country.

civilization: a group of people, or society, that has made advances in government, science, or the arts.

clan: a group of people descended from the same ancestors.

coca: a leaf chewed by the Incas in order to kill pain or stimulate the body. Today it is made into a dangerous drug called cocaine.

convent: a building where nuns, women who have vowed to live a religious life, live.

creator: a being or god believed to have made the universe.

crowbar: a strong metal bar used as a lever.

decimal system: a method of counting based on tens.

empire: a collection of conquered or allied states, ruled over by a single government.

excavate: to dig up.

granite: a hard rock, often used for building.

irrigation: a system of watering the soil for growing crops.

litter:	a vehicle for carrying passengers. It is fitted between two handheld shafts.
llama:	a grazing animal of South America. It is used for carrying heavy loads, and for providing wool.
mamacuna:	unmarried women who vowed to live religious lives and serve in the temples.
masonry:	the stonework of walls or buildings.
mortar:	a mixture of lime, sand, or cement, used to bind together bricks or stones.
niche:	a recess or compartment in a wall.
osteologist:	a person who studies bones.
panpipe:	a musical instrument made up of sections of cane, each with a different length and note.
prefect:	an official or governor.
quinine:	a valuable medicine taken from the bark of certain shrubs and trees that grow in Peru.
quipu:	a system of knots and cords, used for counting and keeping coded records.
radiocarbon dating:	measuring the rate of radioactive decay in an object, in order to date it.
ransom:	a payment demanded for the safe return of a captive.
ritual:	a religious ceremony.
saddle:	a ridge of land joining two mountain peaks.
schist:	a form of rock that contains shiny crystals.
social classes:	divisions in a society based on wealth or power.
story:	a floor or horizontal section of a building.
survey:	to take exact measurements of the land or of a site.
tax:	a sum of money or tribute paid by an individual to the government, in return for services received. The Incas did not use money, so citizens paid in produce or labor. In return, they were well cared for by the government.
textile:	cloth made by weaving.

Index